THE GOLDEN AGE
OF HANDBUILT BICYCLES

TEXT: JAN HEINE
PHOTOGRAPHY: JEAN-PIERRE PRADÈRES

A Life Filled With Passion Is a Life Well Lived

May you always follow your passions.

Love
Cath
2005
Christmas

VINTAGE BICYCLE PRESS
SEATTLE

Index

*During the early post-war years,
many randonneurs participated
in competition. Here Lyli Herse leads
Lucien Détée (right) and R. Martinez (left)
as part of the winning team in the Coupe
René Herse 1951, a 100 km (62 mile)
team time trial.
Photo courtesy L. Détée.*

Preface

Cycling for the enjoyment of riding and exploring has a long history on many continents. In France, Paul de Vivie, better known by his pen-name Vélocio, started a movement at the end of the 19th century that espoused riding long distances, in any weather, over any terrain – because it is fun. This "School of St. Etienne" had a profound influence on cycling and bicycle design in France.

Today, most developments in cycling are inspired by racing, but that was not always the case. In the early days, racing bikes usually had only one speed and ineffective brakes. Racers did not mind walking up hills as long as their competitors were similarly handicapped. But this would not do for the so-called cyclotourists – "real-world" riders – who insisted on riding up the steepest mountain passes simply to see "what is on the other side of the mountain." As a result, they developed lightweight bicycles with multiple gears, powerful brakes, and useful lights. Their pride in their sport made them demand beautiful, well-crafted machines that were as elegant as they were reliable. Slowly, some of that technology trickled down to mass-produced bicycles, but the custom-built machines from the "constructeurs" always stood head and shoulders above the rest.

Because their manufacture was so labor-intensive, these wonderful bicycles were made in small shops who turned out a few dozen, maybe a hundred machines in a year. These were bicycles that cost the equivalent of three month's professional salary in the early post-war years. They were very rare when they were new, and they are much rarer today. Every detail was carefully designed and fabricated. Fenders and racks form integral parts of the bike, so nothing will rattle, rub or come loose. Every part is attached to a brazed-on fitting, because clamps can loosen and slide out of position. Lighting wires run inside the frame. This not only makes for a cleaner, more elegant bike, but the wires also are protected from being snagged and broken. Different from framebuilders, the constructeurs built completely integrated bicycles. They made their own stems, front derailleurs, brakes and even hubs when they were not satisfied with the performance or esthetics of the parts available commercially. These bikes achieved a level of craftsmanship that never has been surpassed.

As the editor of *Vintage Bicycle Quarterly*, I have been lucky to see many wonderful machines. For this book, photographer Jean-Pierre Pradères and I have travelled far and wide on two continents to photograph some of the most amazing bicycles the world has seen, to chart the history of French handbuilt cyclotouring bicycles. I hope you enjoy this voyage into a world when bicycles were the stuff of dreams and legends.

Jan Heine

1910 - 1939
The Formative Years

By 1910, bicycles had evolved into the shape we recognize today: A "diamond" frame, two wheels of equal size, and chain drive. For racing, where flat courses dominated, these machines were the epitome of modern technology, with lightweight butted tubes and quality components. But for cyclotouring, the available machines, with a single speed and ineffective brakes, still were inadequate. Uphill, riders needed multiple gears to ride where they wanted to go. Downhill, they needed reliable, powerful brakes.

As a result, the next two decades were dedicated to the perfection of gear changing mechanisms and brakes. Various systems to obtain variable gears were tried before the derailleur generally was accepted (in France) as the most efficient solution. By 1930, cyclotouring bikes had evolved to feature multiple gears, useful brakes, fenders and lights.

But a small group of cyclotourists, the Groupe Montagnard Parisien (Paris Mountaineering Group) still were not satisfied. Why, they asked, do cyclotouring bikes weigh up to 20 kg (44 lbs.)? Why are they difficult to steer around curves at high speeds? And why are our outings marred by breakdowns of various components?

To change all this, they organized a "Concours de Machines" in 1934, a "technical trial," where not riders, but bicycles competed against each other. Points were given for light weight, front derailleurs and other desirable features. Points were deducted for anything that broke or did not function perfectly after 460 km (288 miles) on rough mountain roads. The trials were a resounding success. While few of the established mass producers participated, a number of young constructeurs entered superlight bikes. To everybody's surprise, these machines held up to the demanding conditions. The winning Barra weighed only 10.35 kg (22.8 lbs.), lighter than most similar machines even today. The trials and subsequent publicity in the cyclotouring press showed the public that light machines and lightweight parts not only were available, but also were reliable.

Because of this success, the technical trials became an annual event. They were sponsored by the trade association of aluminum manufacturers, who wanted to promote the widespread use of aluminum parts in bicycles. This goal was achieved: By 1938, quality cyclotouring bikes featured cranks, hubs, handlebars, rims and many other parts made from aluminum – even aluminum frames in some cases. During the 1930s, encouraged by the publicity available through the technical trials, numerous young constructeurs opened shop and perfected their designs.

At the same time, profound societal changes were taking place in France. After years of labor unrest, French workers obtained a mandatory 40-hour workweek and two weeks of paid vacation for every employee. For the first time, workers had leisure time. With very little money and a great desire to enjoy nature, tens of thousands explored the countryside on bicycles on weekends and during their vacations. The Golden Age of cyclotouring had begun.

Lucien Guibert with his R.P.F. bicycle in 1928:
One of the best cyclotouring bicycles available
at the time.
Photo courtesy R. Henry.

La Gauloise
Bi-Chaîne 1909 - 1910

La Gauloise
Bi-Chaîne 1909 - 1910

Starting in the late 1880s, Paul de Vivie, better known as Vélocio, went on long non-stop rides of forty hours or more, covering vast distances for the enjoyment of cycling and seeing the countryside.

Much of France is hilly or mountainous, so Vélocio became an early proponent of multiple gears. Before reliable derailleurs were developed, there were numerous systems to obtain multiple gears. The "Bi-Chain" was one of them.

Vélocio owned a bicycle shop, where he built bikes based on frames from various manufacturers. He incorporated gearing systems and brakes of his own design, and sold the bikes under his brand-name "La Gauloise."

The "Bi-Chain" concept is simple: Either one or the other chain are engaged by pressing the foot lever on the right-side crank, giving two speeds. In addition, each side has two freewheel sprockets and two chainrings, providing two extra gears. To change these gears, the chain is opened using special quick release links (see detail photo), a length of chain is removed (or added), and the chain is placed on the other combination of cog and chainring.

There is only one brake, which is activated by backpedaling. It slows the rear wheel. The handlebars can be turned around after removing the faceplate on the stem, to give a more sporting position. For its time, this was an amazingly versatile machine that allowed riders to follow their dreams to the end of the road.

Hirondelle
Rétro-Directe 1920s

The Manufacture Française d'Armes et Cycles began to produce bicycles in 1886. Three years later, they took over another maker, Hirondelle ("Swallow"). Bicycle production grew steadily, until the company counted some 5,000 employees in their factories during the 1930s. Hirondelle bicycles were known as quality products, well-proven and not likely to follow short-lived fads.

The "Rétro-Directe" was listed in the Hirondelle catalogue from 1903 until 1939. The gear mechanism is remarkably simple: The chain is wound in a figure-eight around two freewheels (of different sizes). One freewheel is engaged when pedaling forward, the other when backpedaling. To change gears, one simply reverses the pedaling motion and pedals backwards.

This top-of-the-line Hirondelle also was equipped with the first commercially available front derailleur. With two chainrings, this gives four speeds that can be shifted while riding.

In the 1920s, the "Rétro-Directe" had many proponents, who claimed that backpedaling used different muscles and thus prevented fatigue. At a time when numerous methods of changing gears were developed, the "Rétro-Directe" was one of the more popular ones.

Schulz

1935 - 1937

Schulz
1935 - 1937

By the 1930s, a market had evolved for bicycles that were a cut above the standard mass-produced machines. Discerning cyclotourists wanted custom sizing and geometries, as well as special features that set their bikes apart from the rest. The constructeur Jacques Schulz from Colombes near Paris was happy to oblige. He had invented a "flexible" bike frame that was supposed to be more comfortable than others. Starting in 1935, he advertised this model and a tandem built on the same principle.

Schulz was a prolific inventor: In addition to the remarkable frame design, he developed extremely powerful brakes and an indexed derailleur called the "Funiculo." The lightweight rims of this bike were made from folded aluminum sheet and riveted along the center. Brake cables were routed through the frame, and the rear rack was quickly detachable by unscrewing two wingnuts. Custom-made pedals and many other parts complement this amazing machine. With so many special parts crafted by hand, Schulz' bikes were expensive, and only very few were made.

Reyhand
1936

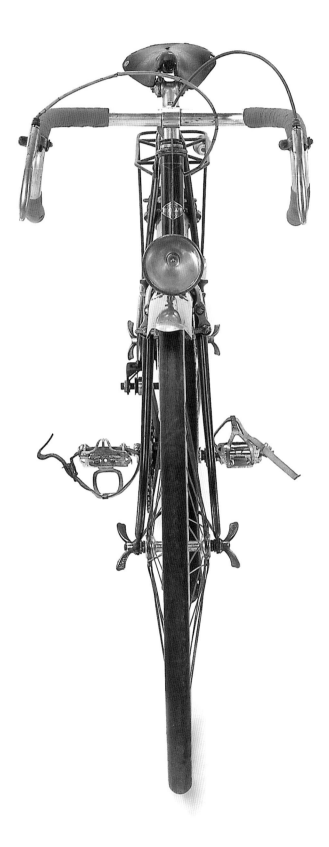

Reyhand
1936

In 1934, a wave of excitement splashed through the French cyclotouring world. A small group of riders from Paris, the Groupe Montagnard Parisien (Mountaineers of Paris), had decided that they were not happy with the heavy, lumbering mass-produced bicycles of the time. To change things, they organized a "Concours de Machines" (technical trials), where bicycles competed for the prize of the best cyclotouring machine.

The technical trials were a resounding success. Cyclists learned that bicycles could be lightweight, nimble and durable. The trials also provided small makers with much-needed publicity for their products. One of these young constructeurs was A. I. Reiss from Lyon. A mechanic and bike dealer, he began building cyclotouring bicycles when the technical trials were announced in 1934. His Reyhand bicycles won the event three times in a row from 1935 to 1937.

At the 1937 technical trials, A. I. Reiss (right) and Gustave Darchieux adjust the bicycle of Germaine Darchieux, winner of the women's category. Photo Paul Bussy, courtesy R. Henry.

Because of the publicity generated by the technical trials, customers started making their way to Lyon, ready to pay a very high price for a superior bicycle. The bike shown here, purchased new by a Docteur Vieu from Toulouse near the Spanish border, shows the incredible progress brought about by the technical trials.

With relatively short chainstays and a relatively steep head angle (for the time), the geometry of the fillet-brazed frame is thoroughly modern, setting a standard that would remain valid for decades to come. Weighing only 11 kg (24.2 lbs.) fully equipped, it features Mavic aluminum rims, powerful Jeay brakes, and a C.A.R. bottom bracket with adjustable cartridge bearings. The AVA seatpost incorporates the saddle clamp. Aluminum was used for the handlebars, stem and chainrings, while the steel Duprat cranks are hollow to save weight.

The frame incorporates a lightweight rack made from steel tubing. A Cyclo four-speed derailleur shifts reliably. Front derailleurs still were considered a superfluous extra, as shifting the chain with one's fingers worked just as well.

Docteur Vieu chose well when he bought this machine in 1936. There was none better, and few have surpassed it since.

Uldry
1936

During the 1930s, cyclotouring – best translated from the French as "riding for the enjoyment of riding" – became very popular. Young Frenchmen and -women wanted to experience nature, to go camping, and to see the country. Cycling combined all these elements at an affordable price. Every weekend and holiday, these enthusiastic riders took to the roads.

In 1929, Monsieur Uldry began making handbuilt custom bicycles in Paris. His bikes were of high quality and well-regarded. In 1934, Uldry participated in the first technical trials. His bikes featured many of the innovations of the 1930s, such as modern geometries, aluminum rims, Cyclo derailleurs and the popular speedometers. This bike is equipped

with a detachable rack and an oiler hole on the seat tube to lubricate the bottom bracket. It was a classic machine of high quality for discerning riders.

Longoni
Super Tandem 1936 - 1937

Longoni
Super Tandem 1936 - 1937

After years of strikes and civil unrest, French workers achieved their goal in 1936: a mandatory 40-hour work week and 14 days of paid vacation for every employee. Most of France rejoiced (except perhaps some owners of factories and businesses). During their new-found spare time, French workers and employees wanted to leave their congested, polluted cities to explore the country and enjoy nature.

Train tickets were expensive, and cars were not even a dream yet for the masses, so tens of thousands took up cycling. They loved the freedom of riding toward the horizon, the challenge of climbing mountains, and the excitement of seeing views they did not know existed. Many bought tandems to enjoy riding as a family. A child-seat mounted on the rear top tube was a popular option. With panniers and sometimes even a trailer, they took to the road, free and full of joy.

Most of these riders had more enthusiasm than money. A custom bicycle from one of the small constructeurs vying for attention in the technical trials was out of the question. For most, a heavy mass-produced machine had to suffice. But some could afford a machine that was a bit better-made, a bit lighter and a lot more reliable.

Around 1930, Charles Longoni began to make beautiful production bicycles that offered 90% of the performance and esthetics of a custom machine at roughly half the cost. This tandem is typical of his best machines. Its age is unknown, but it corresponds exactly to the descriptions in the 1936/37 Longoni catalogue. The

fork-mounted speedometer/odometer shows only 7727 km (4830 miles).

The cable-operated Rosa front derailleur shifts reliably over the wide range of gears. The Jeay brakes plus the rear drum provide ample stopping power. The well-braced frame is made from seamless Durifort tandem tubing. It is adequately stiff for a family of three. Even the weight of 25 kg (55 lbs.) is acceptable for a fully equipped touring tandem. But most importantly, it cost 1,975 francs, when a top-of-the-line Reyhand (see p. 36) tandem was almost twice as expensive at 3,885 francs.

Holidays in the Alps, 1936.
Photo Lucien Thimonier, courtesy R. Henry.

Reyhand
1938

Reyhand
1938

In the 1930s and 1940s, cycling was a popular sport for well-situated enthusiasts. A beautiful custom bicycle was a status symbol, and cyclists discussed the merits of various components and materials just like they do today.

When Henry Chaix from Lyon, who had been a friend of Vélocio, decided to buy a new bicycle in 1938, he chose a Reyhand. These machines built by A. I. Reiss had assumed almost mythical status among well-informed cyclotourists, and they fully deserved their fame. Every Reyhand was a masterpiece. Monsieur Chaix simply wanted the best bicycle money could buy, so he checked every available option on the order sheet. The resulting bicycle assured him the admiration of his peers.

The bike is equipped with three shift levers. The one on the top tube controls the Cyclo rear derailleur, and the one on the left of the down tube shifts the Simplex front derailleur. The lever on the right of the down tube adjusts the spring tension of the rear derailleur. Many people believed that excessive spring tension on the derailleur would cause significant drag on the chain.

This bike also features internal routing for the rear brake cable. The C.A.R. hubs and bottom bracket are equipped with adjustable cartridge bearings. The superlight aluminum rack is inspired by the lightweight machines of the technical trials. But Monsieur Chaix was more concerned with comfort than weight, and mounted his beloved, heavy Brooks saddle with large springs, which already had graced his previous bike.

Henri Chaix with his Reyhand.
Photo courtesy R. Henry.

Intégral
1938 - 1939

Intégral
1938 - 1939

The 1920s and 1930s were a time of great experimentation in bicycle design. Many were not yet ready to accept the standard diamond frame and continued to look for improvements. Around 1923, Monsieur Bachelier introduced his Intégral bicycles, which featured numerous novel ideas. Most striking are the twin down and the seat tubes. Bachelier placed the chainrings between the seat tubes to reduce the load on the bottom bracket. The hub bearings are housed inside the dropouts, which also spreads the load. All bearings can be removed without tools by opening a lever on the bearing housing. This makes maintenance and even bearing replacement a snap.

Oval chainrings – to smooth out the pedal stroke – have been tried time and again throughout the history of bicycles. But sometimes innovation can go too far: Originally, this bike was equipped with prototype brakes that did not work well. So after a few months, the bike was sent back to Bachelier, who replaced the brakes with standard Jeay calipers.

Bachelier appears to have faded from the cycling scene with the onset of World War II. One wonders whether some of his ideas, such as the easily accessible hub bearings in the dropouts, do not merit another look.

Reyhand
1938 - 1939

In addition to thousands of cyclotourists who used their machines to travel and enjoy the country, there were those with more sporting ambitions. The fastest times and records for various long-distance rides were coveted among the randonneurs. Many quickly discovered that a good tandem team can be significantly faster than a single rider.

These "tandemistes" needed the best equipment. The frame of this top-of-the-line Reyhand tandem, made from oversize Reynolds 531 tubing, is well-braced and stiff enough even for strong teams. All components were chosen for light weight and durability, resulting in an impressively low weight of 18 kg (39.6 lbs.) fully equipped. The brake lever for the rear Idéal drum brake can be locked to prevent speed from building up on unpaved mountain descents. Together with the front Jeay brake, the braking power was sufficient. The tandem never had a rear rim brake, although the builder provided braze-ons just in case.

Painted in Reyhand's house color of brown with orange pinstripes, this tandem remains completely original, down to the handmade, superlight Barreau "Mouette" 650B x 42 mm tires.

1940 - 1959
The Classic Age

When the German army invaded France in 1940, everyday life changed from one day to the next. Food was in short supply. Skilled workers feared deportation to work in German armament factories. Jews faced a fate even worse than that.

Despite the incredible hardship, bicycle production continued on a limited scale. While many of the big factories were converted to armament production by the Germans, the small constructeurs continued to build their amazing machines. Parts were traded on the black market, and somehow these intrepid makers managed to keep their shops running.

Compared to the general population in Paris, cyclotourists were at a great advantage. Procuring supplies in the region became increasingly difficult, so they took to the road in search of food. Riding 400 km (250 miles) on a weekend, they were able to roam far and wide, trading goods from the city for vegetables, meat and flour. It was a hard time, but the enjoyment of cycling could not be suppressed. Competitive events, such as the famous Poly de Chanteloup hillclimb race, continued even during the war, and new, shorter events took the place of long rides that were impossible due to curfews and the division of France into the "Occupied" and the "Free Zone."

Once France had been liberated by the Allied troops, it did not take long for the cycling world to spring back. The first technical trials were organized less than a year after the war. Most of the constructeurs reopened their shops: Narcisse returned from the "Free Zone," Alex Singer came out of hiding, René Herse moved to larger premises, Nicola Barra returned to continue making his aluminum bikes, and Jo Routens started a new shop in his hometown of Grenoble. Names like Derche, Daudon and Ducheron stood for beautiful, carefully conceived bicycles. But many others, including A. I. Reiss, maker of Reyhand bicycles, had perished in the war.

During the post-war years, bicycles were more than just transportation or sports equipment. Similar to an expensive sports car today, a custom bicycle was the ultimate status symbol at a time when cars were rare and unaffordable, when housing was in short supply, and when foreign travel was difficult. Influenced by the technical trials, many people aspired to own a superlight bicycle with special features. There were "Concours d'Elegance," where riders in outfits custom-tailored by famous "couturiers" showed off their equally elegant bicycles.

Custom bicycles were more popular than ever before. New constructeurs opened shop every year. But this Golden Age did not last long. With the advent of affordable motorized transportation – first mopeds and motorcycles, then the famous Citroën 2CV and Renault 4CV cars – bicycles rapidly went from status symbol to poor people's transportation. A recession in the mid-1950s didn't help, and by the late 1950s, only a few die-hard enthusiasts were buying expensive custom bicycles. But while it lasted, the Golden Age produced some marvellous machines.

Henri Decker (front) and Gilbert Bulté on a Rémy tandem during a time trial in 1950. Photo courtesy Mme. Goyon.

Charrel
1945 - 1946

Only well-earning professionals could dream of a hand-made custom bicycle during the 1930s and 1940s. It is no coincidence that most of the constructeurs worked in Paris. Lyon, the second-biggest city in France after Paris, provided enough of a customer base to support a few builders. Here, Paul Charrel made some wonderful machines.

This bike was made for Charrel's brother-in-law. The fillet-brazed frame features interesting details, such as a relatively narrow fork crown and internal routing for brake and derailleur cables. Charrel also made his own cantilever brakes and the superlight rear rack. The resulting bicycle weighs only 10.3 kg (22.7 lbs). It rivals the products of the best constructeurs from Paris.

Alex Singer
1946 - 1947

Like many of the second generation of constructeurs, Alex Singer had been riding for other makers in the 1930s technical trials. In 1939, he began to build bicycles on his own in Levallois-Perret, a suburb of Paris. He immediately made a name for himself by setting records for light weight at the technical trials of 1939.

His bikes built on that reputation. Many features set them apart from those of other constructeurs, from a special support for the Cyclo derailleur made from four small-diameter tubes to the superlight front derailleur. The resulting bikes were impressively light. This one weighs 10.5 kg (23.1 lbs.). It is painted in the metallic blue that was Singer's signature color at the technical trials.

*After World War II, Alex Singer (center)
was joined by his wife Maria (right)
and his nephew Ernest Csuka (left)
at the shop at 53, rue Victor Hugo.
Here they pose during a ride in 1946.
Today, the original shop is tended by
Ernest Csuka, the last constructeur to make
cyclotouring bikes in the old tradition
(see p. 129).
Photo courtesy E. Csuka.*

René Herse
Concours de Machines 1947

René Herse
Concours de Machines 1947

Suspense was in the air at the 1947 technical trials. The previous year, the team of René Herse had suffered numerous failures due to hastily prepared equipment. With their reputation on the line, the small team of René Herse pulled out all the stops and produced some truly impressive machines.

Every detail was reworked in search of a few grams saved. The front derailleur was made from aluminum, with a shortened lever. The cranks and chainrings were filed and reduced to an absolute minimum. Pedal cages were cut away, brake levers filed and even the pump was shortened to save weight. Because the extremely thin lower pump peg bends easily, the pump was mounted upside down! A superlight aluminum low-rider rack held the bags for the 4 kg (8.8 lbs.) of luggage the bikes had to carry.

The frame was made from superthin 3/10 mm Reynolds 531 tubing (standard is 7/10 mm), fillet-brazed to eliminate the weight of the lugs, with a special twin-plate fork crown and ultra-thin dropouts. Even the derailleur spring was shortened. The saddle was modified extensively, and it bolts directly to a special seatpost. Of course, all bolts were machined from aluminum. The result was an impressive machine weighing just 7 kg (15.4 lbs.). The bikes were weighed without tires and innertubes to level the playing field, because lightweight tires were available only on the black market so shortly after the war. The complete bike therefore weighed about 7.9 kg (17.4 lbs.), including fenders, lights, rack and pump.

To prevent riders from riding too gingerly on the rough roads, speed counted in the results. René Herse assembled a team of fast, but careful riders. The result was a convincing victory, with the first four places among the men, the first place among the women, and the best tandem all going to Herse.

It is amazing that a machine from the 1947 technical trials has survived almost completely intact. A few parts have been changed and replaced (see page 164), but essentially, the bike is as it was ridden in 1947.

Follis

Type Polymultiplié 50
Chanteloup 1946 - 1947

In the mid-1940s, the French sports papers considered Roger Billet "the king of cyclotourists." Obviously, the sports writers did not understand that cyclotouring is a democratic sport. While there may be some competition, every cyclotourist is valued the same, because the ultimate goal is to enjoy the ride. But this misunderstanding should not diminish the athletic achievements of Roger Billet. He beat the record for the climb of the Mount Ventoux, which was held by the professional racer René Vietto. Billet also won the randonneur event of the Poly de Chanteloup in 1945 for Singer and in 1946 for Follis. Still for Follis, he participated in the 1946 technical trials. Hampered by many flats due to faulty tires, the Follis bicycle took last place, but Billet had shown his class by riding away from the field.

In 1903, François Follis began making bicycles in Lyon. At first, he concentrated on racing bikes, even sponsoring a professional team. During the late 1940s, Follis branched out into cyclotouring bikes. Billet's competition successes may have helped, but the quality of the bicycles was more important to obtain sales among discerning cyclotourists. The "Type Polymultipliée 50 Chanteloup" is very similar to Billet's bike from the 1946 "Poly." The choice of 700C wheels shows the maker's racing heritage, as does the rack made from steel wire, which lacks the elegance and light weight of the tubular racks made by the small constructeurs.

But Follis knew how to make bikes, and quality components, such as Sécurite cantilever brakes (the company later changed its name to Mafac), complement a nice frame with internal cable routing and chrome-plated head lugs. Superlight cork brake pads are the finishing touch on a classy machine.

René Herse

1946 - 1947

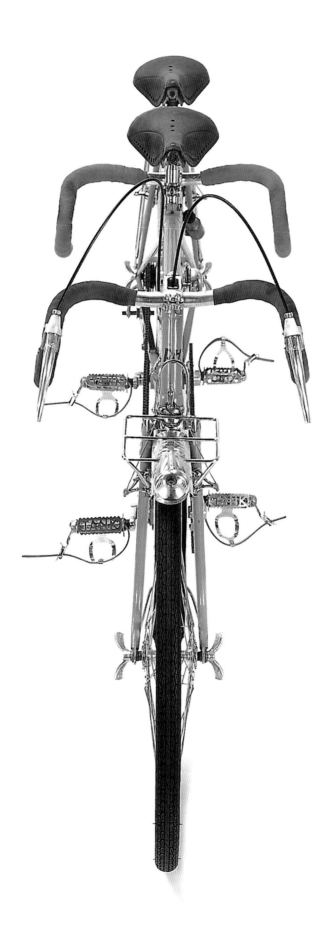

René Herse
1946 - 1947

Randonneurs are amateurs who ride long distances for the joy of cycling. Their crown jewel is Paris-Brest-Paris, a ride across France over 1200 km (750 miles). This event started in 1891 as a professional race. Since 1931, there has been a separate category for randonneurs. Even though the randonneurs are amateurs, and their goal is to complete the ride in less than 90 hours, there always has been a healthy dose of competition among them. Trophies and records for fastest in various categories are coveted to this day.

In 1948, the famous illustrator Daniel Rebour and his wife Simone set out for an unusual honeymoon trip: They set a new mixed tandem record in Paris-Brest-Paris. Their machine was a René Herse tandem similar to the one shown here. Herse was an experienced tandem rider himself, and his "bicycles built for two" were revered for their quality and precise handling.

The tandem shown here spent 15 years in a shed before it was found in early 2003. Restored over a couple of months, it was pressed into service for the 2003 Paris-Brest-Paris ride. After 52 hours and 45 minutes of riding almost non-stop, it returned to Paris as the first mixed tandem, ridden by the author of this volume and Jaye Haworth. The 55-year-old René Herse once again had proved its worth in the face of competition on modern machines made from titanium and carbon fiber.

*Many René Herse tandems were used
in competition. Here, Jean Dejeans
and Paulette Callet descend at speed
in the 1943 Poly de Chanteloup hillclimb race
on their way to second place.
Photo courtesy Paulette Porthault.*

Alex Singer
1947

When Monsieur Bernick ordered a new bicycle in November 1947, he already owned at least one Alex Singer. But this one was going to be special – the lightest bike one could buy. At the technical trials in 1946, Alex Singer had set a record for the lightest cyclotouring bike. That incredible machine weighed only 6.875 (15.16 lbs.), a record that was not even broken by the superlight Herse machines at the 1947 trials (see p. 44). So Monsieur Bernick went to Singer for his new dream bike.

Alex Singer at the 1946 Technical Trials with his bike weighing 6.875 kg (15.16 lbs; without tires). The bags hold the required 4 kg (8.8 lbs) of luggage.
Photo courtesy E. Csuka.

The frame was fillet-brazed from thin-walled 5/10 mm Reynolds 531 tubing, and every detail was specified as light as possible. Mavic fenders were lighter than the popular "hammered" Lefols. The rear rack was made from lightweight aluminum tubing instead of steel. The already superlight Singer cam-actuated brakes were drilled and filed. Even the wingnuts have large holes to save a few precious grams. Details include a fork crown machined underneath and fender attachment bolts filed to a minimum. The resulting bike weighed approximately 10.2 kg (22.5 lbs.) – impressively light for such a large machine with a 60 cm frame. But it still was a far cry from the machines of the technical trials, which shows how impressively light those bicycles were thanks to their extensively modified components.

Mayeux
Cyclosportif late 1940s

"Cyclosportifs" are what Americans would call "century riders:" Cyclists who take to the road every weekend and enjoy entering organized events to challenge themselves. Unlike randonneurs, many cyclosportifs do not ride at night, so their bikes do not need lights. And they like to go fast, so their equipment choice tends more toward racing bikes.

This Mayeux combines the best of racing bikes with the best of randonneur bikes. Equipped with 700C x 30 mm tires, it rides like a racing bike, but features the much-superior parts of a cyclotouring bike: a reliable Cyclo rear derailleur, a modified Simplex front changer, and Maxi-Car hubs.

Fifteen speeds help conquer any hill, and powerful cantilever brakes

ensure safety on the descents. The second shift lever on the right adjusts the chain tension. To save weight, there is no seatpost. The modified Idéale saddle with alloy rails is mounted directly onto the extended Vitus seat tube.

The complete bike is a very lightweight machine, tipping the scales at a scant 10.0 kg (22.0 lbs.). At the time, racing bikes with cranks, derailleurs, stems and seatposts made from steel, easily weighed an extra kilogram or two.

Mayeux was a small builder in Paris, who started building either before or during World War II, and vanished from the scene in the 1950s.

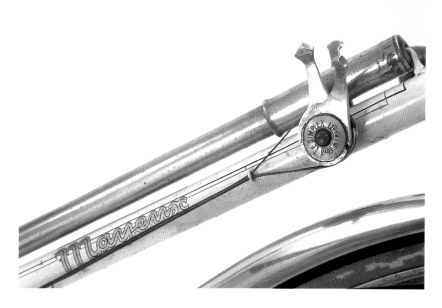

Alex Singer

Porteur ca. 1947

At the Alex Singer shop in 1945
(l. to r.): Mr. Briseau, Roland Csuka,
Mr. Nagy, Ernest Csuka, Mr. Dugit.
Photo courtesy E. Csuka.

Alex Singer
Porteur ca. 1947

In the 1930s, Alex Singer had been a racer. Like many racers, he liked to ride a fixed gear during the winter months, so he built this bike as a fixed gear training bike. Later he modified it into a "porteur," a bicycle to carry parcels to and from the post office. But it also was a machine he could use on the rides of the newspaper carriers – the "porteurs" – many of whom raced on weekends and used their paper delivery routes as training (see p. 92).

The frame is fillet-brazed at the rear, but lugged at the front. Headlugs and head tube have been welded together to form a single piece, which was a Singer trademark. The rack Singer made for his "parcel carrier" is lighter than those of the true "porteurs," which were designed to carry 50 kg (110 lbs.) of newspapers.

The fabric chainguard saves additional weight. The Maxi-Car hubs have been modified with large flanges riveted to the hub shells, another

Singer specialty. Singer's cam-actuated brakes and a seatpost with an internal expander complete this impressive machine, painted in the Singer house color "Bleu Foncé." Even on the way to the post office, Alex Singer could be proud of his bike.

Maury

Late 1940s

The late 1940s saw a return of prosperity in France. A custom bicycle showed that "one had made it." The shinier and the more elaborate it was, the more impressive. Fully chrome-plated frames were popular. Special components and features commanded the same attention as special wheels and "V12" engines do among today's car enthusiasts.

Many constructeurs competed for these image-conscious customers. André Maury began to make cyclotouring bicycles in 1932. He participated in the first technical trials in 1934, where his bikes came second and third, laying the foundation for his excellent reputation.

Photo courtesy S. Rebour

Maury's bikes always were innovative. The custom stem was clamped
between the upper headset cup and
the locknut, predating the current
Aheadset system by at least 40 years.
The Speedy cantilever brakes were
introduced in 1938, when they were
considered a revolution in stopping
power and modulation.

The elegant chainguard indicates
that the bike was intended more for
city riding than for true cyclotouring
exploits. Without a front derailleur,
shifting from one chainring to the
other requires stopping the bike and
moving the chain by hand. It is possible
that the bike originally was equipped
with only one chainring, and that a
second one was added later to update
the bike when double and triple
chainrings became popular.

But not all Maury bicycles were
ridden by urban sophisticates. The
photo on the left shows Simone
Rebour, wife of illustrator Daniel
Rebour, on top of the Galibier with her
Maury.

L. Pitard
1948

In 1949, the original owner of this bike went to the shop of Louis Pitard. Even though Pitard's "boutique" was located in the red-light district of Paris, he had gained a reputation for solid quality bikes since 1928. The customer wanted a custom bike, but he wanted it soon, to take on his summer vacation. That posed a problem: Pitard's order books were full and the waiting list was long.

Louis Pitard asked the customer whether a used bike in perfect condition might work. He took a rather special bike from the wall and explained that it had served in the Poly de Chanteloup hillclimb race that year. It was as good as new, and it fitted the customer perfectly. So the customer bought it on the spot, happy to have a bike in time for his vacation.

The bike he bought was rather special compared to Pitard's usual machines. It is equipped with lightweight brakes made by Marcadier (see p. 100). Pitard made a superlight front derailleur and brazed the alloy rails of the saddle directly onto the seatpost to eliminate the saddle clamp. But Pitard always erred on the side of durability, and even his "superlight" bike weighed 11.5 kg (25.3 lbs.).

Despite having been ridden extensively – including commuting every day – the bike is in great condition. To prevent it from being scratched or stolen in the communal bicycle garage, its owner carried it up seven flights of stairs every night to park it in his apartment.

Juliette and Louis Pitard after completing their third Paris-Brest-Paris, 1951. Photo Maurice Berton, courtesy of R. Henry.

A. Faure

Ca. 1948

A. Faure
Ca. 1948

Monsieur Faure was a watchmaker in Saint Etienne. Apparently, he was an avid cyclotourist, who built his dream bikes on the side. He may have made several bikes, but only one is known today.

The bike shown here features many interesting details. Monsieur Faure started out with carefully filed lugs and a hand-made twin plate fork crown, but the frame's sloping top tube shows a certain lack of experience.

An exceptional amount of work has been lavished on the components. Bolts, rack and fender stays, as well as other small parts have been custom-made. Because Monsieur Faure considered holes and threads unsightly, he plugged every hole that normally appears on various components: The Stronglight cranks now hide the pedal axle ends, the wingnuts are closed, and specially made domed nuts disguise the threads usually visible on the derailleur rod, shift lever and other components.

The rear reflector has been modified to incorporate the taillight. Looking down on the stem, the rider sees a harmonious ensemble of matching bell, pocket watch and speedometer. By applying his incredible skills, Monsieur Faure brought the concept of a fully integrated, completely custom bicycle to its logical conclusion.

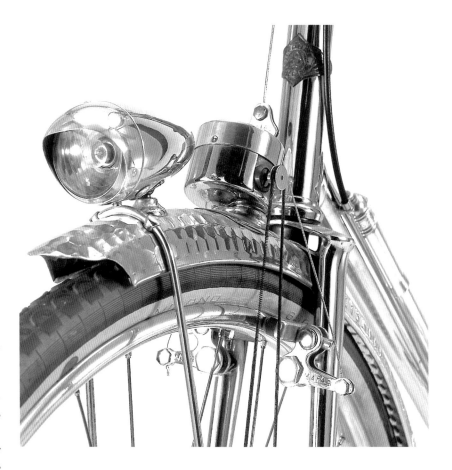

René Herse
Camping 1948

THE GOLDEN AGE OF HANDBUILT BICYCLES

René Herse
Camping 1948

Many well-off cyclotourists saw camping not as inexpensive accommodation, but as the ultimate expression of the cyclotouring philosophy: Ride where you want to go, free from the need to find a bed to sleep and food to eat. After climbing mountain passes all day, pitch your tent in a meadow along the way, cook your dinner on a small stove, and watch the stars alight in the sky – what better way to explore a region, a country, the world?

For those who chose camping by design rather than necessity, the constructeurs offered carefully designed "camping" bikes that often exceeded their other machines in sophistication and cost. Reinforced frames were equipped with sturdy racks made from steel tubing. Carefully chosen components ensured that the bikes were reliable, yet reasonably lightweight. The bike shown here weighs only 13.3 kg (29.2 lbs.) fully equipped.

The rear drum brake allows braking on long mountain descents without overheating the rims. This is especially important when descending on loose gravel. As was usual on the best Herse bikes, all lighting wires run inside the frame, from the generator through seatstay and rear fender to the bottom bracket. The wire continues through the downtube and via a carbon brush in the headset to the front fender and finally to the front light. The special light mount is hollow, and the cable runs through it. The light itself is placed far forward to be out of the way of a load on the front rack.

The original owner, Monsieur Morisot, used this marvellous machine

only sparingly and carefully. When it was found more than 50 years after it had been built, everything except the tires remained as it had been in 1948, down to the original toestraps. After a thorough clean, and fitted with period tires, it presents itself like it would have in Herse's shop in 1948.

Hugonnier
Routens
Ca. 1949

Paul Barbier was a wholesaler of bicycle parts in Saint-Etienne. His business was going well. He followed the Tour de France in his huge Buick, a true symbol of ostentation at a time when even a modest Citroën 2CV was only a dream for most people. For his personal bike, only the best would do: the comfort and sophistication of a true randonneur bike.

To obtain this machine, Barbier went to Jo Routens. Routens was a well-known rider who had participated in the technical trials. He had won many randonneur events, including the Poly de Chanteloup and Paris-Brest-Paris. When Routens set up his shop in Grenoble in 1945 together with his business partner Hugonnier, his reputation was such that serious riders from all over southern and eastern France considered his machines.

Barbier was an important customer, and Routens made a very special bike. In addition to the typical features, such as the seatstays attached to the top and seat tubes, and the cable routing for the rear brake through the seat tube, this bike features an elegant twin-plate fork crown. The lower plate extends into a small ornamental tang on the fork blade, a feature usually found only on Routens' personal bikes. Barbier obtained a number of special parts from A. Faure (see p. 66) to dress up his bike, including the elegant, adjustable front light mount and various screws and bolts. The resulting bike was one which an important wholesaler of bicycle parts could ride with pride.

C. Bailleul
Ca. 1950

Claude Bailleul was an active cyclotourist. Less is known about his activity as a builder of bicycles. Few of his machines survive. This one is a well-conceived machine using the best components throughout.

The expensive Stronglight cranks lived up to their name: Forged from aluminum, they were stronger than most steel cranks, but much lighter. The adapter for the triple chainrings was a desirable option because it allowed changing chainrings without removing cranks or pedals. A Cyclo rear derailleur and a Huret front changer shift reliably over all 12 speeds. Maxi-Car hubs, Bell wingnuts, Lefol "Le Paon" fenders and an Idéale saddle complete this quality machine.

French law required that riders displayed their name and address on the bike. Most riders had a simple stamped bronze plaque riveted to the frame, but that would not do for a custom bike. Bailleul engraved the information on the TA cable guide, while others put it on the stem cap or even the stem itself.

Charrel

Ca. 1950 - 1953

Historic photos of Paris-Brest-Paris and other competitive events rarely show women's bikes. Most sporting women preferred the lighter weight and improved stiffness of "men's" frames. But many women's bikes were built for riders who were not quite ready to straddle a top tube.

After some experiments with twin lateral tubes, most constructeurs adopted the labor-intensive frame design shown here: A single diagonal tube is joined at the seat tube by two extra stays. These frames rode as well as men's bikes.

This Charrel illustrates the craft of its builder. The clean fillet-brazed frame is well-proportioned. The cables for rear derailleur and rear brake run inside the frame tubes, with a small roller on the seat post binder to route the cable to the rear brake.

René Herse
Randonneuse 1950

Many considered René Herse the best and most innovative of the constructeurs. A look at his career helps explain how he achieved that stature.

On September 2, 1930, the French aviators Coste and Bellonte landed their Breguet airplane with the apt name "Question Mark" in New York. They were the first to cross the Atlantic against the prevailing winds, only three years after Charles Lindbergh's pioneering flight in the other direction.

At the Breguet aircraft factory, a young "mécanicien" named René Herse had worked extensively on the "Question Mark." As an avid cyclotourist, Herse realized that many bike parts could be improved with the new technologies used in aircraft design.

When the Breguet factory was shut down by the labor unrest of 1936, Herse quit his job and began making lightweight bike parts, including aluminum stems, pedals and cranks. Complete bicycles followed in 1940, equipped with many special parts of his design. Each component was as elegant as it was functional, whether the superlight cantilever brakes, the beautiful cranks, the unique stems, the special light mounts or the custom-made screws and bolts.

Every Herse was different: This one was built for a rider on the Herse team. It features very thin fork blades usually found on Alex Singer bikes. The bike is all original down to the Wolber tires.

Alex Singer
1950

THE GOLDEN AGE OF HANDBUILT BICYCLES

Alex Singer
1950

With so many constructeurs competing for orders, the annual "Salon du Cycle" in Paris was very important, even though it was not open to the buying public. If a builder's new feature or design caught the discerning eye of the journalists, the result was free publicity, which translated into orders.

When Ernest Csuka, nephew of Alex Singer, needed a new tandem, it was decided that this machine would be the "show bike." The tandem was equipped with the best Singer had to offer, including his cam-actuated brakes, the superlight front derailleur and the reliable Nivex derailleur. The bike also featured two internal expander seatposts. The stems were a special model with a triangular point at the front. The stoker stem was brazed onto the front seatpost. A remote control on the seatstay operated the generator.

Originally painted in the characteristic "Bleu Foncé," (see p. 58) the tandem was much-admired at the "Salon." Daniel Rebour showed several of its innovative features in his drawings, which were published in various magazines. After being a showpiece, the tandem was put to good use. Ernest and Léone Csuka were avid randonneurs, who competed in many events.

In 1953, the tandem was stripped and overhauled to be exhibited at the "Salon" once again. This time, the frame was chrome-plated. Fresh from the "Salon," Ernest and Léone Csuka went to Belgium, where they participated in the "Poly de Huitzingen" tandem race (overleaf). In the decades since, it has seen many rides. Today, it is owned by Ernest and Léone's son Olivier, who continues to enjoy it.

Ernest and Léone Csuka
at the Poly de Huitzingen race near Brussels,
Belgium, in 1953.
Photo courtesy Ernest Csuka.

Barra

Ca. 1950

Barra

Ca. 1950

Cyclists always have been fascinated by light weight. With the limited power output of the rider, every gram saved is one gram less to accelerate from a standstill, and one gram less to haul up the hills. The technical trials of the 1930s succeeded in showing that a good bicycle does not need to be heavy. Within a short time, the weight of the best cyclotouring bikes had dropped to only 11 kg (24.2 lbs.), but how light could one go? Would there be, some day, a 5 kg bike?

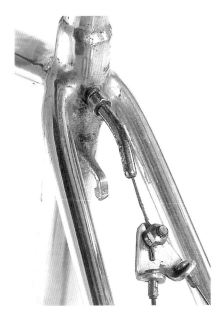

Nicola Barra's name comes up time and again in the quest for light weight. He won the first technical trials in 1934. In the 1936 trials, he tied for first with Reyhand. The winning bike was made from thin-wall steel tubing, but Barra also introduced a frame brazed from aluminum tubing at this event. Many cyclists saw this as the material of the future, and Barra soon specialized in making aluminum frames.

Barra's role as an innovator did not end with aluminum frames. He also developed the first modern cantilever brake in 1936. The bike shown here, made around 1950, is equipped with a later version of the brakes. The toe-in of the brake pads can be adjusted, a feature not found on most bikes until the 1980s.

Racks made from aluminum tubes and a Barra front derailleur complete a machine that weighs only 9.5 kg (20.9 lbs.), fully equipped. It is hard to imagine a lighter bike equipped with standard components.

René Herse
Porteur 1950

René Herse
Porteur 1950

The "porteurs" delivered the morning and afternoon papers to newsstands across Paris. The tool of their trade was the "porteur" bicycle. The more discerning among them ordered custom bikes from the great constructeurs, not only because these bicycles rode well, but also because the quality construction meant that after a long day at work, these porteurs did not have to repair their bikes.

Many of the porteurs were bicycle racers, who trained "on the job." Once a year, there was the "Championship of the Porteurs," where competitors had to carry huge stacks of newspapers

The start of the Porteur Race at Blvd. Montmartre/Paris, in April 1958. The course went over 38 km (23.75 miles), and each rider carried 15 kg (33 lbs.) of newspapers.
Photo X.

across Paris, exchange their packages and return to the start. Riding in a peloton of porteurs over the cobblestones of Paris at 45 km/h (28 mph) must have been exciting, to say the least.

A typical porteur bike was characterized by its huge front rack, guaranteed to carry 50 kg (110 lbs.) day after day. This bike is special even among the rare Herse porteurs. Ten speeds and a cable-operated Herse front derailleur helped climbing the many hills of Paris. A superlight saddle and a freewheel that stays in place when the rear wheel is removed, are expensive special touches. The original owner must have been a successful porteur who knew what he wanted in his dream bike.

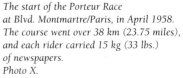

C. Daudon

Randonneur 1950 - 1951

C. Daudon
Randonneur 1950 - 1951

Camille Daudon's shop was located near the famous Champs Elysées in Paris, not far from the famous "haute couture" boutiques of Chanel and Dior. In his advertisements, Daudon called himself the "Couturier du Cycle" (Tailor of Bicycles). His bicycles were supremely elegant and well-conceived.

His "Randonneur" model usually had only a curved front rack, but on this bike, both racks follow the curve of the wheels. Originally, the bike was equipped with custom leather bags made specifically for the curved racks by a saddlemaker.

Like many builders at the time, Daudon clamped his custom stem directly to the fork's steerer tube. Inside the steerer tube, he placed a repair kit. After unscrewing the knurled cap on top of the stem, you retrieve an alloy tube containing tire levers, patches and all the wrenches needed to adjust the bike.

Daudon's randonneur bike was designed for comfort and sophistication. Rubber-covered wingnuts, leather-covered toeclips and a long lever on the Daudon front derailleur make using this machine a joy.

Camille Daudon (left)
with his brother-in-law G. Luez,
who rode for the club Daudon sponsored.
Photo courtesy S. Rebour.

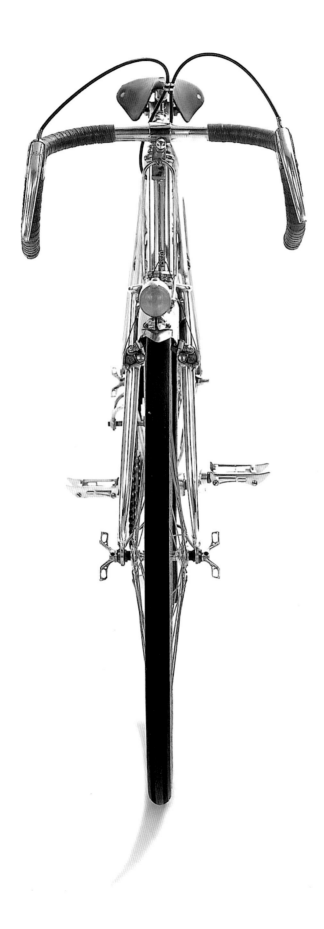

Marcadier
Ca. 1950

André Marcadier had worked in a machine shop, before he began to build bicycles with Jo Imbert in 1947. They made superlight steel and aluminum bicycles under the C.I.M. (Cycles Imbert-Marcadier) brand. But the partnership did not last long, and soon Marcadier worked on his own.

Marcadier's bikes were remarkably light: This one weighs only 9.5 kg (20.9 lbs.) fully equipped. To arrive at such a light weight, every part was carefully selected. The Roger Piel pedals have no ball or roller bearings, but sleeves made from oil-impregnated bronze with oil channels to ensure lubrication. The Dumont alloy-railed saddle saved precious grams. Even the wingnuts for the Exceltoo hubs were cut out.

As much care has been lavished on the presentation, with internal cable routing for the rear brake and the derailleurs, including even the spring of the Cyclo derailleur.

A. Rémy
Ca. 1951

Rémy started selling mass-produced bicycles in 1913, with frames made by various manufacturers. Soon Rémy became one of the largest bicycle dealers in Paris. In the 1940s, the daughter of the original founder married Maurice Goyon, who was an avid cyclotourist. The couple took over the business.

Starting in 1948, Goyon branched out to build fine cyclotouring bikes. His motto was "Au petit qui n'a pas peur des grands" (The small one who isn't afraid of the big ones), which alluded his goal to compete with the "big" constructeurs like Herse and Singer.

The bike shown here is typical of a Goyon's best bikes. The Remy front derailleur was crowned by a lucky dice. The Leno brakes were designed by André Noël, a rider on the Rémy team. He made them on the side while working for the Lockheed brake company.

Special touches include a single-tube support for the Cyclo rear derailleur and a seatpost with internal expander. Instead of a front rack, the bike features a single tube that supports both the handlebar bag and the front light.

With some competition successes thanks to his friends, Goyon carved out a small niche for his bikes, before becoming a victim of the bicycle market's downturn. The Rémy store was sold in 1955 or 1956, and the production of high-end bikes ceased.

The Rémy team at the 120 km time trial of the Vélo-Club de Courbevoie-Asnières, 1950 (left to right): Pierre Mirate, André Noël, Gilbert Bulté, Henri Decker. Photo courtesy Gilbert Bulté.

Caminargent

Ca. 1951

Caminargent
Ca. 1951

Pierre Caminade introduced his "all-aluminum" Caminargent bicycle in 1936. It was a masterstroke. The aluminum tubes were inserted into slotted cast aluminum lugs. Tightening the four-sided "Allen" bolts locked them in place.

The concept was designed for series production. The head tube, complete with imitated lugs, was cast in one piece. Unlike steel frames, there was no filing, brazing or painting required. Frames were available in several sizes and could be equipped as track, racing, randonneur or city bikes. There even was a ladies' model.

The tubes of the Caminargent were octagonal, and to complement this, the racks were made from octagonal tubing as well. Some bikes even had octagonal fender stays! A single tool allowed disassembling the entire bicycle. Caminade also made rims, stems, brakes, wingnuts, and even saddles, all of which equip the bicycle shown here.

The early Caminade bikes with few accessories and only 3 or 6 speeds were remarkably light. However, this bicycle made in 1951 had additional features that brought the weight up to 11.4 kg (25.1 lbs.) – no lighter than a steel bike.

C. Daudon
Cyclosportif 1951

In the 1940s and 1950s, there were numerous competitive events for cyclotourists. Many builders sponsored clubs, who organized time trials, brevets and even track races. The competition was friendly, but hard-fought. The main difference to "amateur" racing was that cyclotourists did not aspire to make racing their livelihood. Like many amateur racers today, they simply enjoyed riding their bikes and competing for the fun of it.

This bike is equipped with 700C x 30 mm tires, LAM sidepull brakes and relatively large gears, as would befit a racing bike. Most events required lights, fenders and a bell (here mounted under the saddle). On cyclosport bikes, Daudon always used a clamp-on version of his hand-made front derailleur, perhaps to allow changes in chainring sizes. This lovely bike combines the pace of a racing bike with the durability and practicality of a randonneur machine.

Paul Thiébaud dedicated this photo
to Simone and Daniel Rebour in 1951.
Photo courtesy S. Rebour.

toute ma sympathi
a mes grand, ami
Simonne & Daniel
tour 5?
Paul

René Herse
1952

René Herse
1952

René Herse built this bike for the "Salon du Cycle" in October 1952. Even among René Herse bikes, it stands out for its elegance and many special features.

The round fork blades and twin-plate fork crown were a special option found on only few bikes. The front rack attaches to the fork crown, stem and fork blades. It incorporates a quick release for the handlebar bag. The rear rack has double eyelets at the bottom, which sandwich the dropouts, to make a stronger connection.

The hubs are equipped with Herse's special extra-large flanges. When the rear wheel is removed, the freewheel remains in the frame, so the rider avoids having to touch the chain when repairing a flat tire. Both hubs have quick-release skewers instead of wingnuts. The bike is equipped with the first TA pedals, which were introduced in 1952. Equipped with needle and ball bearings, these pedals were so astronomically expensive that very few were sold. This was a dream bike in 1952.

*Lyli Herse on the way to set a record
in the Puy de Dôme hillclimb, 1948.
Photo courtesy L. Herse.*

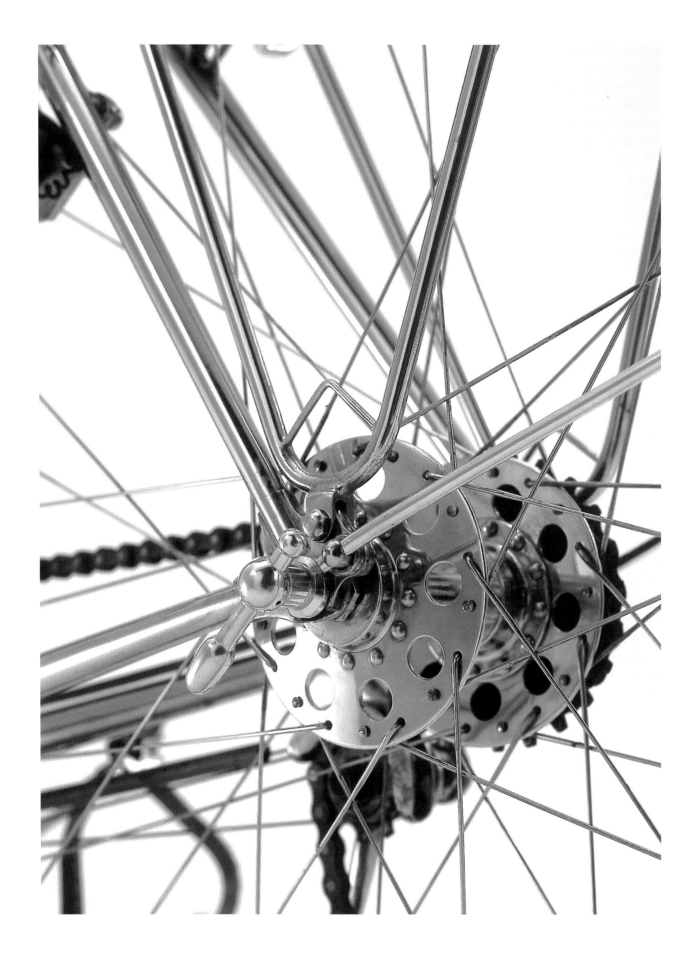

THE GOLDEN AGE OF HANDBUILT BICYCLES

Longoni
Campeur ca. 1950

Some bikes are beautifully preserved because they have not been ridden much. In contrast, this Longoni camping bike has a great history, which expresses itself in wonderful patina. Badges and pennants are witnesses of rides and places visited. The rider reinforced the lighting wires and replaced the bar tape as it wore out.

Even though Longoni did not make custom machines on par with the best constructeurs, this bike features internal cables and a chain oiler that uses the seat tube as a reservoir. Steel cranks and other "budget" parts kept the price affordable without affecting reliability on the open road. One can imagine this bike in travel photos from exotic places.

Marcadier

1950s

Marcadier
1950s

Making a good tandem is much more difficult than a single bike. Not only are there more parts, but the forces of two strong riders pedaling in unison are enormous. André Marcadier had a good feel for materials, and his bikes were amazingly light and durable. This tandem weighs only 17 kg (37.4 lbs.) with a heavy drum brake, lights, fenders and a front rack.

The frame is made from oversized, ovalized aluminum tubing. Like many of the best constructeurs, Marcadier made special parts for his bikes. Many constructeurs made their own stems and front derailleurs, but Marcadier also developed very sophisticated cam-actuated brakes, which push the pads straight toward the rim. The pedals on this tandem have bearings on one side only, with the platform lowered to improve biomechanical efficiency.

When bicycles fell from fashion in the 1950s, André Marcadier went on to build racing karts. Soon, a rule change required a minimum weight of 50 kg when Marcadier's karts weighed only 27 kg! Refusing to weigh down his creations with ballast, he went on to design sports cars, turning out a number of very successful creations.

Alex Singer
1953

In his youth, Ernest Csuka was a strong rider. In 1945, he placed 8th in the Poly de Chanteloup hillclimb race. In the 1950 "Tour de France Cyclotouriste," he won two stages. This race went over the same course as the professional event, but the stages were neutralized until the last 50 km, when the real racing started.

One might think that the constructeurs always rode new bicycles, but that was not usually the case. Either they were too busy to build bikes for themselves, or there simply was too little money to afford yet another machine.

*Ernest Csuka (center) won
the stage to Grenoble
of the 1950 Tour de France Cyclotouriste.
Alex Singer is on the right.
Photo courtesy E. Csuka.*

This is the bike of Ernest Csuka, the current owner of Cycles Alex Singer. It was made in 1953. Originally, it was equipped with Singer brakes and a Nivex derailleur. The bike has been updated several times with new components. Today, Ernest Csuka continues to ride it on most weekends with his club.

Barra
1950 - 1955

The "mixte" frame of this aluminum Barra belies the fact that this bike is a serious performance machine for an experienced rider.

The owner must have had confidence that her saddle height was not going to change, because there is no seatpost. The superlight saddle clamps directly to the extended seat tube. The stem also clamps directly to the steerer tube.

The complete bike weighs only 10.5 kg (23 lbs.) fully equipped with a wide range of gears and two lightweight racks made from aluminum tubing.

1960 - 2005
The Tradition Continues

Cars became affordable in the 1950s, and cycling lost its universal appeal. As a result, most of the constructeurs closed their doors. Others, like Alex Singer, adapted by selling various sporting goods to augment the meager income from custom bicycles. But even if fashion had left cycling by the wayside, the sport of cyclotouring survived. Randonneurs continued to ride their brevets. Paris-Brest-Paris saw more participants than ever before. Even if most French dreamed of a new car with tailfins, cyclotourists continued to dream of wonderful bicycles. And the remaining constructeurs were happy to turn these dreams into steel and aluminum.

Around 1970, the American bike boom took the cycling world by surprise. Almost overnight, demand for bicycles vastly outpaced supply. Suddenly, anybody who could supply frames was in business. At the top end of the market, a few hundred Alex Singers and René Herses found their way across the Atlantic Ocean. It did not take long for the fitness movement to reach France, and cycling once again became popular.

In the 1940s, randonneur bikes had been the epitome of technology, but now racing bikes were becoming increasingly popular. As a result, cyclotouring bikes of the 1970s incorporated many racing bike parts. This was possible, because racing bikes finally had caught up to cyclotouring bikes with respect to gear ratios, lightweight components and reliability. Paradoxically, bikes became heavier because most of the extralight components no longer were available.

The renaissance of the handbuilt cyclotouring bike in the 1970s also was its swansong. A generational change was under way among the constructeurs. Jo Routens, René Herse and others retired. Building bicycles by hand is hard work and does not bring riches. In most cases, the children of the constructeurs had little interest in keeping the shop open. Today, of all the old names, only Cycles Alex Singer remains. Here, Ernest Csuka continues to craft wonderful bicycles in the tradition of the "Golden Age of Handbuilt Bicycles."

Ernest Csuka (right)
and his son Olivier at Cycles
Alex Singer in 2004.
Compared with the photo on page 59,
not much has changed in 59 years.
Photo J.P. Pradères

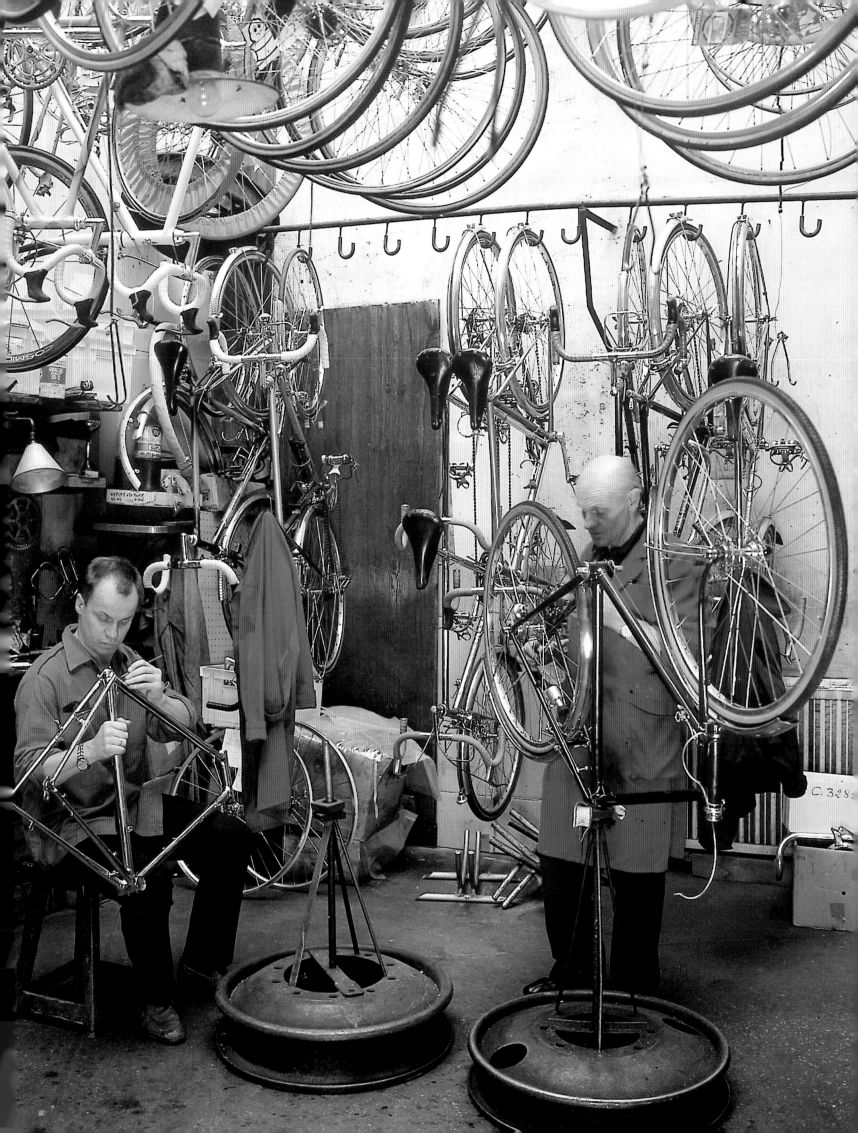

Goëland
Campeur 1961

Louis Moire had been selling cyclotouring bikes under the name "Goëland" (Seagull) since 1935. His motto was "La marque du juste milieu" (the brand of the middle ground). Most Goëland bikes featured nicely crafted frames, but were equipped with mid-level parts to arrive at a price that was significantly less than that of a bike from one of the "top" makers.

This bike was built for loaded touring. It is equipped with the best and newest components available at the time. The cottered TA aluminum cranks were introduced the same year this bike was built. They combine the narrow profile of steel cranks with the light weight of aluminum. With a bike like this, there is little need to aspire to more than the "middle ground."

Alex Singer
1962

Alex Singer
1962

There are those who do not believe that new always is better. Monsieur Kahlen ordered this bike in 1962 as a retirement gift to himself. He already owned several Alex Singer bikes. His new bike looks more like an Alex Singer from 1952, with classic components throughout: a Nivex rear derailleur, Singer lever-operated front derailleur, Singer brakes and a chainrest on the rear dropout. The superlight Mephisto rims feature wooden reinforcement blocks under each spoke nipple. Monsieur Kahlen also specified every option that set Alex Singer bikes apart: head lugs welded onto the head tube, a bottom bracket with cartridge bearings, an internal expander seatpost and a remote-control lever to operate the generator.

During the early 1960s, the Singer shop had few orders, often making no more than 15 bikes in a year. It is obvious that extra care was lavished on this bike for a favored customer. The filing of the lugs is even crisper than usual. Special touches include an extra-long lower point on the seat lug that forms the base for the pump peg. The bike rides like a dream, and the derailleurs shift as well as any. One can see why Monsieur Kahlen preferred the tried and true.

René Herse
Paris-Brest-Paris 1966

On a clear September night in 1966, Maurice Macaudière and Robert Demilly crouched over their bikes as they raced toward Paris, on the return leg of Paris-Brest-Paris. They already had ridden 1000 km (625 miles) across France and back, but Paris still was far. The two teammates had dropped all other randonneurs. They were on schedule to set a new record for the 1200 km (750 mile) event.

As the morning dawned after their second night on the road, their René Herse bicycles continued to run like clockwork, but the riders felt the efforts of their record-setting pace, compounded by a lack of sleep. First Demilly weakened. Macaudière slowed

THE GOLDEN AGE OF HANDBUILT BICYCLES

*Maurice Macaudière (left) and Robert Demilly
arrive at a control toward the end of
their record ride in Paris-Brest-Paris 1966.
Behind the bikes are Lyli and René Herse.
Photo courtesy M. Macaudière.*

and pulled him along for many kilometers. Then, on one of the last hills before the finish, Macaudière suffered terribly. He had to stop and rest for a while. But he, too, recovered.

The two returned to Paris in triumph, 44 hours and 21 minutes after they left. This was a new record, at an average speed of 27.1 km/h (16.9 mph), including stops. For the fifth time in as many PBP events, René Herse won the "Challenge des Constructeurs" (Builder's Trophy) for the five best-placed riders.

One might think that a winning ride in Paris-Brest-Paris requires a very special, superlight bike. But Maurice

Macaudière's machine from 1966 is as standard as it gets for a René Herse. The only concession to the long-distance event are two eyelets on the front rack. Here, a flashlight was attached at night to provide illumination without the drag of a generator. For such a small bike, Macaudière's machine is on the heavy side at 12.2 kg (26.8 lbs.), but reliability and comfort were more important than light weight.

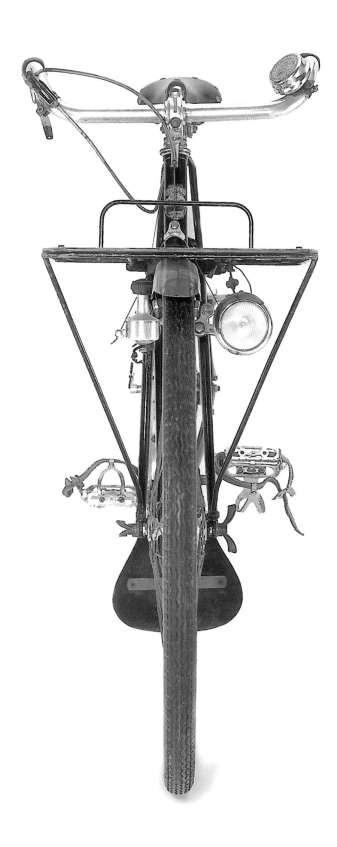

Goëland

Porteur ca. 1966

In the 1960s, this Goëland was one of the nicer porteur bikes you might have seen in Paris. Imagine it appearing on one of the "Grands Boulevards," deftly weaving in and out of traffic, the front rack stacked up to the handlebars with newspapers.

For ease of maintenance, the bike is equipped with an internally geared Torpedo 3-speed rear hub and cartridge bearings in the bottom bracket. Rims, fenders and pedals are made from steel for durability. Carefully crafted and not without a certain elegance, it lacks any unnecessary frills. A true workhorse for a demanding job, day after day.

Jo Routens
1966

In 1952, Jo Routens left the partnership with Hugonnier (see p. 74) and set up shop on his own. He continued to build his exquisite fillet-brazed randonneur bikes and tandems, even if the bulk of his sales were mass-produced bicycles bought from outside suppliers.

This elegant bike is one of the rare top-of-the-line cyclotouring machines Routens built. It features some typical Routens details, such as the triangular reinforcements on the bottom bracket shell, twin-plate fork crown, hand-made cable-operated front derailleur and rear brakes mounted ahead of the seatstays.

The minimal rear rack is less typical for Routens' bikes, but it is no less elegant. Production of the Cyclo derailleur had stopped around 1960,

but upon special request, Routens equipped new machines with older parts.

René Herse
Démontable 1971

frame 100 ← 135 →

In these publicity photos from 1962, René Herse demonstrates the very first "Démontable" in front of his shop. The shop window lists the first five of the eight French championships his daughter Lyli won throughout her professional cycling career. Photos courtesy L. Herse.

René Herse
Démontable 1971

At the Paris bike show,
René Herse exhibited his "Demontable"
in the trunk of a car.
Photo courtesy L. Herse.

In the 1960s, a small group of cyclotourists in the United States formed the "International Bicycle Touring Society." Their leader was Dr. Clifford Graves, a surgeon from La Jolla, California. Through contacts with the French youth hostel movement, Graves discovered the wonderful bikes of René Herse. Not being very mechanically inclined, he admired the maintenance-free hubs, bottom brackets and other quality features. They allowed him to enjoy riding in remote locations without having to fear breakdowns. He spread the word, and soon a steady trickle of René Herse machines found their way across the Atlantic Ocean.

Cyclists used to travel by train when they were not astride their machines. In the 1960s, cars became increasingly popular. At the German Bicycle Show in 1960, various makers presented small-wheeled folding bicycles that fit into the trunk of a car. This was the start of a folding bike craze that swept over Europe for the next decade.

René Herse rose to the challenge by offering a fully equipped randonneur bike with a frame that split into two pieces. The front section of the top tube fits into the rear section and is secured by a quick release. The downtube sections are joined with a sliding sleeve. A special quick release stem and slotted cable guides facilitate disassembly, as do shift levers that are located on the seat tube. The generator/light on the front wheel is a self-contained unit, complemented by a battery-powered taillight.

This bike was ordered as one of a pair by Mr. and Mrs. Meinke of Germantown, Ohio. They were avid bicycle tourists, so their bikes were equipped with a large rear rack and removable flanges on the small front rack, allowing each to carry four panniers.

René Herse
Porteur 1975

By the 1970s, trucks delivered the newspapers in Paris. The proud profession of the "porteurs" had died out. But there were others who required a bike to carry large loads. In addition to the typical front rack, this porteur can be equipped with a large rear rack, making it a true beast of burden.

The current owner uses the bike everyday in Paris to run errands. He reports that it rides as well as it looks.

Alex Singer
Campeur 1985

While one constructeur after another closed their doors for good, Ernest and Roland Csuka continued to build bikes in the great tradition of Cycles Alex Singer.

The original owner of this bike intended to travel far and wide, so he ordered a very special camping bike. In addition to a reinforced frame, it features heavy-duty racks and two rear brakes. Unfortunately, his travel dreams never were realized, and the bike saw little use.

After its owner's death, the bike went on an Odyssey around the globe before finding a new home. With its stiff frame and sturdy racks, this bike is easy to ride even with 35 kg (77 lbs.) in the four panniers. Now it awaits a bicycle tour of the South American Andes. The dream lives on.

René Herse
1978

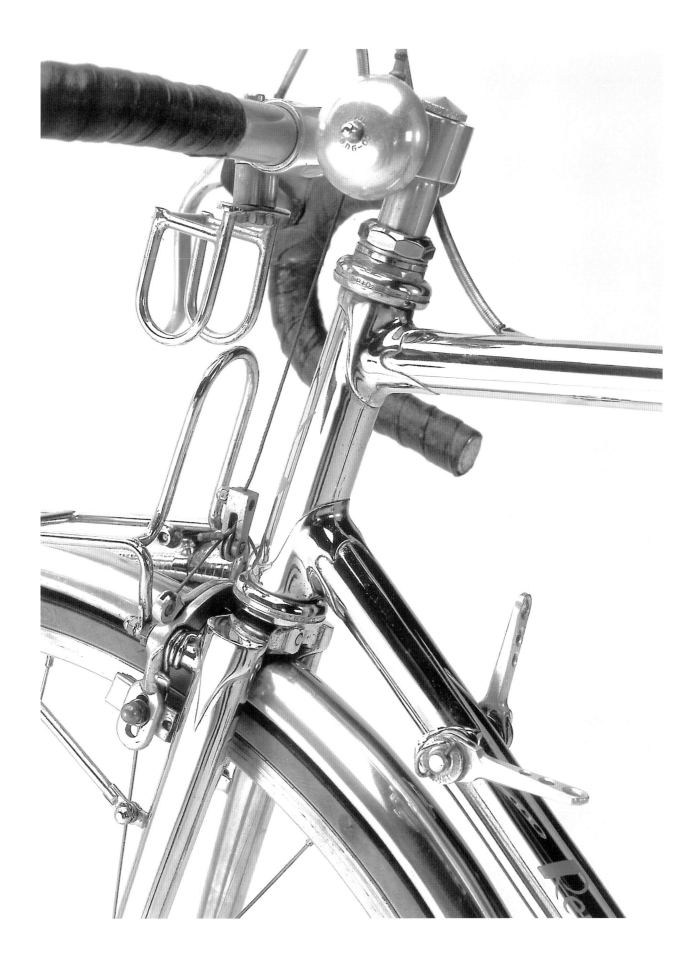

René Herse
1978

After René Herse died in 1976, his daughter Lyli and her husband Jean Desbois took over the shop and continued to turn out the same marvellous bikes as before. Quality and finish were excellent, and the waiting list was long. It was a sad day for cyclotourists when the Herse shop closed in the mid-1980s.

This bike is equipped with battery-powered front and rear lights for night-time riding. The standard generator-powered system serves as a backup. Additional features include round fork blades and a twin-plate fork crown. The shift lever on the seat tube operates the generator. With sure-stopping Weinmann centerpull brakes on special brazed-on pivots and reliable Huret derailleurs, this bike combines the elegance of the old machines with 1970s technology.

Gilles Berthoud
1980

The young constructeur Gilles Berthoud began to build custom bicycles in 1977. In 1985, his shop took over the production of the popular Sologne bags, which had equipped cyclotouring bikes for decades. Today, they continue to be available (see p. 151), still sewn by hand from fabric and leather.

This tandem was Berthoud's personal machine. It graced his stand at the 1980 Paris Bicycle Show.

René Herse
Tandem Chanteloup 1980

René Herse

Tandem Chanteloup 1980

In 1962, Madeleine and Daniel Provot won the tandem race of the last Poly de Chanteloup for René Herse (left). Photo courtesy L. Herse.

The tandem race of the "Polymultipliée de Chanteloup" hillclimb was a very prestigious event in the 1940s and 1950s. For more than a decade, René Herse's daughter Lyli dominated the event with various partners. In 1958, René Herse introduced a tandem with a curved seat tube similar to those offered by the British framebuilder Claud Butler and others. The shorter wheelbase made the tandem corner better and also may have improved out-of-the-saddle climbing, but at the expense of a bumpier ride for the stoker (rear rider).

Long after the demise of their namesake event, "Chanteloup" tandems

continued to show the finest craftsmanship of the René Herse shop. Each lug was made by hand from pieces of tubing welded together, because oversize tandem lugs were not available. The twin-plate fork crown and internal cable routing show the hand-writing of Jean Desbois, who built this amazing machine. The tandem rides as well as it looks. It is equally at ease on out-of-the-saddle climbs as on fast, curvy descents.

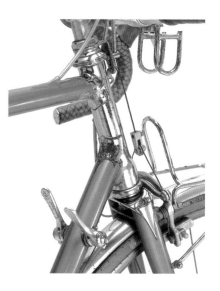

Alex Singer
2003

At Cycles Alex Singer, Ernest Csuka continues to build amazingly beautiful and functional bicycles. Many are traditional, equipped with parts no longer made. But he also makes bikes which combine the convenience of the new with the practicality and reliability of the old.

On this randonneur bike, a modern Campagnolo "Ergopower" drivetrain and clipless pedals are mated to Mafac centerpull brakes (for fender and rack clearance) and classic TA cranks (for unlimited selection of chainring sizes). Its owner, a former racer, prefers this machine over all his others, for its combination of light weight and performance.

Ernest Csuka sets up a frame on the jig in 2004.

1910 - 2005

Originality

Most of the bikes in the previous pages are at least 40 years old. For this book, we have selected bikes that are as original as possible. Almost all have their original paint. The few exceptions are bicycles whose historic significance merits their inclusion even if they have been repainted.

As far as possible, the bikes are equipped with the parts they carried when new, but some items, especially tires, usually are replaced several times over the active life of a bike. During the 1950s and 1960s, there was a trend toward narrower tires. A number of bikes in these pages are equipped with these later, smaller tires, and "air" shows between fender and tire. The collectors who care for them today have preferred to keep the narrow tires, which match the patina of the bike. Other owners have installed current-production tires with the correct dimensions, but which do not match the weathered finish of their bikes.

Because we would like this book to serve as a reference for how these bicycles were equipped originally, the list below details the non-original parts – as far as we know – for each bike. We also list the serial number, approximate tire size and approximate weight (where known).

1910 - 1939
- La Gauloise **Bi-Chaîne, 1909 - 1910**: 14.2 kg (31.2 lbs.).
- Hirondelle **Rétro-Directe, 1920s**: 16.2 kg (35.6 lbs.).
- Schulz **1935 - 1937**: 14.8 kg (32.6 lbs.). Tires smaller than original, front light missing.
- Reyhand **1936**: 650B, 11 kg (24.2 lbs.). Tires smaller than original, generator, front rim not original.
- Uldry **1936**: 650B. Light, generator not original.
- Longoni **Super Tandem, 1936 - 1937**: 650B x 42mm?, 25.0 kg (55 lbs.). Tires smaller than original.
- Reyhand **1938**: No. 1238: 650B x 42 mm, 12.5 kg (27.5 lbs.). Rear rim, cranks not original.
- Intégral **1938 - 1939**: 650B. Brakes were replaced shortly after it was built.
- Reyhand **Tandem, 1938 - 1939**: 650B x 42mm, 18 kg (39.6 lbs.).

1940 - 1959
- Charrel **1945 - 1946**: 650B x 35mm. 10.3 kg (22.7 lbs.). Lights may not be original.
- Alex Singer **1946 - 1947**: 650B x 42mm, 10.5 kg (23.1 lbs.). Tires smaller than original.
- René Herse **Technical Trials, 1947**: 650B x 38mm, 9.0 kg (19.8 lbs.; current weight). Tires smaller than original, front light, rear reflector, straddle cable yoke, rear derailleur, some bolts not original.
- Follis **Type Polymultiplié 50 Chanteloup, 1946 - 1947**: 700C x 28mm. Front and rear lights, as well as handrests on the brake levers probably not original.
- René Herse **Tandem, 1946 - 1947**: No. 308: 650B x 42mm, 18.7 kg (41.1 lbs.). Repaint. Tires, brake levers, rear handlebars, toe-straps, bell and potentially the front and rear lights are not original. Hubs have larger Alex Singer flanges.
- Alex Singer **1947**: No. 613: 650B x 38mm, 10.5 kg (23.0 lbs.; current weight). Bike was rebuilt from a pile of bits. Originally, it had alloy toeclips, hand-made tires, narrower fenders and probably different chainrings.
- Mayeux **Cyclosportif, late 1940s**: 700C x 30mm, 10.0 kg (22.0 lbs.). May have been repainted early in its history.

- Alex Singer **Porteur, ca. 1947**: 700C x 28mm. Bike was modified to porteur by A. Singer.
- Maury **Late 1940s**: 650B x 38mm, 12.0 kg (26.4 lbs.).
- L. Pitard **1948**: 650B x 38mm, 11.5 kg (25.3 lbs.).
- A. Faure **Ca. 1948**: 650B x 42mm, 12.9 kg (28.4 lbs.). Toestraps not original. Lock for rear wheel missing.
- René Herse **Camping, 1948**: No. 109 36 148: 650B x 42mm, 13.3 kg (29.3 lbs.). Pivo bottle cage dates from 1950s.
- Hugonnier-Routens **Ca. 1949**: No. HR939: 700C x 28mm, 12.0 kg (26.4 lbs.). Repaint. Rear rim is not original.
- C. Bailleul **Ca. 1950**: 650B x 42 mm, 12.5 kg (27.4 lbs.)
- Charrel **Mixte, ca. 1950 - 1953**: 650B x 42mm, 12.3 kg (27.1 lbs.). Steel rims and chainring may not be original. Tires smaller than original.
- René Herse **Randonneuse, 1950**: No. 187. 650B x 38mm, 11.3 kg (24.9 lbs.). Rear derailleur probably not original.
- Alex Singer **Tandem, 1950**: 650B x 35mm. Front derailleur changed to post-1956 model. Saddles and other wear-and-tear parts not original.
- Barra **Randonneur, ca. 1950**: No. 4187: 650B x 38mm, 9.5 kg (20.9 lbs.). Tires smaller than original.
- René Herse **Porteur, 1950**: No. 80 50. 650B x 42mm, 13.4 kg (29.5 lbs.).
- C. Daudon **Randonneur, 1950 - 1951**: 650B x 38mm, 12.5 kg (27.5 lbs.)
- Marcadier **Randonneur, ca. 1950**: 650B x 35mm, 9.5 kg (20.9 lbs.). Generator missing.
- A. Rémy **Ca. 1951**: 650B x 38mm, 13 kg (28.6 lbs.).
- Caminargent **Ca. 1951**: 650B x 38mm, 11.4 kg (25.1 lbs.).
- C. Daudon **Cyclosportif, 1951**: 700C x 30mm.
- René Herse **1952**: No. 110 52. 650B x 38mm, 11.9 kg (26.2 lbs.).
- Longoni **Campeur, ca. 1950**: 650B x 42mm. Handlebar tape, reflector not original.
- Marcadier **Tandem, 1950s**: 650B x 38mm, 17.0 kg (37.4 lbs.). Tires smaller than original.
- Alex Singer **1953**: No. 454 (E. Csuka's personal number): 700C x 25mm, 11 kg (24.2 lbs.). Many parts replaced.
- Barra **Mixte, 1950 - 1955**: 650B x 38mm, 10.5 kg (23.1 lbs.). Tires smaller than original.

1960 - 2003
- Goëland **Campeur, 1961**: 650B x 42mm, 14.4 kg (31.7 lbs.).
- Alex Singer **1962**: No. 1179: 700C x 25mm, 11.8 kg (26.0 lbs.).
- René Herse **Paris-Brest-Paris, 1966**: 700C x 25mm, 12.2 kg (26.8 lbs.). Derailleurs not original.
- Goëland **Porteur, ca. 1966**: No. 2224: 650B x 42mm.
- Jo Routens **1966**: No. 2666. 650B x 32mm.
- René Herse **Démontable, 1971**: No. 119 71: 700C x 28mm, 13.7 kg (30.2 lbs.). Tires, handlebar tape not original.
- René Herse **Porteur, 1975**: No. 15 75. 650B x 42mm. Tires, cranks, axle nuts, saddle not original.
- Alex Singer **Campeur, 1985**: No. 2711: 650B x 32mm, 15.9 kg (35.0 lbs.). Repaint, rear light, reflector, stem, handlebars, chainrings and rear racks not original, but made/installed by the Singer shop.
- René Herse **1978**: No. 36 78. 700C x 28mm. Bottle cage, tires not original.
- Gilles Berthoud **1980**: 650B x 32mm, 18.3 kg (40.3 lbs.).
- René Herse **Tandem Chanteloup, 1980**: No. 11 80: 650B x 35mm.
- Alex Singer **2003**: No. 3308: 700C x 23mm, 10.7 kg (23.5 lbs.).

The Authors

Jan Heine is the editor of *Vintage Bicycle Quarterly*, a magazine about classic bikes and cycling history. He has participated in numerous randonneur brevets, including Paris-Brest-Paris. Jan relies on bicycles as his primary transportation in and around Seattle, where he lives with his family. He frequently travels to France to research the history of cyclotouring.

Jan Heine with his 1950s Alex Singer in Seattle.

Jean-Pierre Pradères is a free-lance photographer specializing in motorcycle subjects. His award-winning photographs have been published in many magazines and books, including the Guggenheim Museum's best-selling "The Art of the Motorcycle." An avid cyclotourist, Jean-Pierre owns and rides several of the bicycles featured in this book. He lives in Paris with his family.

Eric Svoboda is a free-lance photographer, who has collaborated with Jean-Pierre on numerous projects during the last 10 years. A motorcycle mechanic by trade, he lives and rides classic bicycles in Paris.

Jean-Pierre Pradères (left) and Eric Svoboda (right).

Photos

Unless noted, all photos in this book were taken by Jean-Pierre Pradères and Eric Svoboda, with a Mamiya RZ 67 medium-format camera, a Mamiya-Sekor 127 mm lens and Fujichrome Provia 100 F RDP III 120 film. Illumination was provided by 6 flash bulbs of 900 and 1200 Joule.

Contributors

Helen March and her father Neville's bicycle collections span the entire history of the bicycle. Helen in particular specializes in bicycles from the Golden Age of cyclotouring. She has researched the histories of several individual constructeurs. Many of the bicycles in this book are from the March collections. The family lives near Bordeaux in France.

Helen and Neville March with one of their favorite bikes (see p. 96).

Raymond Henry has been a cyclotourist since the late 1950s. He knew several of the great constructeurs. Today, he is the head of the Cultural Heritage Commission of the French Federation of Cyclotouring (FFCT). He has done extensive research into the history of French cyclotouring bikes. Many of the bikes in these pages are from Raymond Henry's collection.

Raymond Henry with his 1974 Jo Routens, which he bought new.

Acknowledgments

We thank the numerous people who have helped with the preparation of this book, including:

Gilbert Bulté
Ernest Csuka (Cycles Alex Singer)
Olivier Csuka (Cycles Alex Singer)
Lyli Desbois (née Herse)
Lucien Détée
René Dochler (Rando-Boutique)
George Gibbs II (Il Vecchio Bicycles)
George Gibbs III
Mme. Goyon
Charles Hadrann (Wright Bros Cycle Works)
Rachel Henry
Laurent Jubin
Maurice Macaudière
Alexander March
Joel Metz
Nelson Miller
Paulette Porthault (née Callet)
Jeff Potter
Simone Rebour
Christophe Salem
Barbara Van de Fen

Further reading

- **VINTAGE BICYCLE QUARTERLY** is a magazine about bicycle history, classic bicycles and randonneuring. The focus is on French cyclotouring bikes, their riders and culture. Past issues have covered the technical trials, the history of Paris-Brest-Paris, Cycles Alex Singer, René Herse and other constructeurs. The magazine has featured catalog reprints, technical details of bicycles featured in this book, interviews with constructeurs and riders, and more. Information from Vintage Bicycle Press or at www.vintagebicyclepress.com

- **CYCLING HISTORY** The Proceedings of the International Cycle History Conference have included articles by Raymond Henry and others on Vélocio (Vol. 2), René Herse (Vol. 4), Jo Routens (Vol. 7), Alex Singer (Vol. 9) and Nicola Barra (Vol. 12). Information from Cycle Publishing, www.cyclepublishing.com.

- **DU VÉLOCIPÈDE AU DÉRAILLEUR MODERNE** By Henry Raymond, 2003: Association des Amis du Musée d'Art et Industrie de Saint-Etienne. ISBN 2-901282-02-4. French-language. An illustrated history of French gear changing systems, including those of the bicycles in this book.

- **THE DANCING CHAIN** History and Development of the Derailleur Bicycle, by Bero F., 2005, 2nd Ed. Van der Plas Publications. ISBN 1-892495-41-4. An illustrated history of gear changing systems from the beginning until today.

EDITOR:
Jan Heine

PHOTOGRAPHY AND CONCEPTION:
Jean-Pierre Pradères with Eric Svoboda

GRAPHIC DESIGN:
Christophe Courbou

First edition
Printed in France

Published by Vintage Bicycle Press
140 Lakeside Ave., Ste. C • Seattle, WA 98122 • USA
Tel: (+1) 206.297.1199
E-mail: jtheine@earthlink.net
Web site: www.vintagebicyclepress.com

Cover photo: 1952 René Herse

Back cover photo: Celebrating at Cycles Hergé (front row, l. to r.):
Jeanine Antonick, Daniel Rebour (with cap),
Mr. Geslin (owner of Cycles Hergé), Jojo Bruillin.
Photo Berton, courtesy S. Rebour.

Publisher's cataloging in Publication Data
Heine, Jan, 1968-
Pradères, Jean-Pierre, 1947-
The Golden Age of Handbuilt Bicycles. First edition.
p: 168. 30.0 cm. Includes bibliographic information.
1. Bicycles and bicycling
2. History of technology
I. Authorship
II. Title: The Golden Age of Handbuilt Bicycles
ISBN 0-9765460-0-0 (hardcover)
Library of Congress Control Number 2005900523